Up Close & Personal
Miley Cyrus
THE UNAUTHORIZED BIOGRAPHY

Lauren Alexander

PUFFIN BOOKS

Published by the Penguin Group: London, New York, Australia, Canada, India,
Penguin Books Ltd, Registered Offices: 80 Strand, London WC2R 0RL, England

puffinbooks.com

First published in the United States of America in *Jonas Brothers: An Unauthorized
Biography* by Price Stern Sloan, a division of Penguin Young Readers Group,
Penguin Group (USA) Inc., 2007
Published in Great Britain in Puffin Books 2008
1

Photo credits: Cover: courtesy of Kevin Winter/Getty Images; Insert photos: first
page courtesy of Steve Ganitz/WireImage.com; second page courtesy of Lester,
Cohen/WireImage.com, Pseudo Imagel/Shooting Star; third page courtesy of
Eric Charbonneau/WireImage.com, Howard Wise/Shooting Star;
fourth page courtesy of Jefferey Mayer/WireImage.com

Made and printed in England by Clays Ltd, St Ives plc

British Library Cataloguing in Publication Data
A CIP catalogue record for this book is available from the British Library

ISBN: 978-0-141-32577-4

www.greenpenguin.co.uk

contents

introduction

The Best of Both Worlds

Zoom lenses in your face. Lights flashing. Reporters shouting out your name. Fans screaming for your attention. It's dizzying excitement that could be hard to deal with – especially if you're just fourteen years old. But if anyone can handle this mayhem, Miley Ray Cyrus can.

Miley's dad is country-singing sensation Billy Ray Cyrus. And when Miley was just a babe, Billy Ray came out with the smash-hit single, 'Achy Breaky Heart'. Having a celebrity parent could be good enough for some kids. You get to bask in their limelight without having to really step out on the stage yourself. But that was not good enough for Miley. She caught the performing bug at the age of two and has never recuperated, which is lucky for us!

Now Miley truly has the best of both worlds – she's the daughter of a mega-celebrity and a rising superstar herself. Miley stars in the wildly successful Disney Channel show *Hannah Montana*. In the show, Miley (her character has the same name) tries to keep her identity as pop star Hannah Montana hidden from her friends and neighbours. On the show, Miley leads a double life – that of the regular kid next door and the hugely popular singer. But it's just all fiction, right?

Well, not exactly – in real life, Miley's two worlds have already collided – but that's a good thing! Miley might play a singer on TV, but she's released two albums, and they're both *huge* hits! On one CD, she sings as Hannah Montana, not Miley Cyrus. But on the other she *is* Miley Cyrus. Sounds complicated, huh? Well, let's take things from the beginning, when Miley was born. And one more thing – she wasn't born Miley Ray Cyrus; she was given a completely different name at birth . . .

chapter 1

A Star Is Born

On 23 November 1992, a little star was born. Her parents named her Destiny Hope. Her mom and her dad, Billy Ray Cyrus, were probably very proud and happy parents. Billy Ray was already basking in the glory of his mega hit 'Achy Breaky Heart', and now he had an adorable baby girl to add to his joy. Her parents named her Destiny because they thought she would go on to do great things. Boy, were they right!

The baby was happy too – and very smiley. Her father nicknamed her Smiley, which was soon shortened to Miley. And the nickname has stuck ever since. When Miley was a baby, some reports say that her mom died. Billy Ray married Leticia 'Tish' Finley on 28 December 1993. Tish is who Miley considers Mom.

Miley grew up in Franklin, Tennessee, USA, a city with a very interesting history. Franklin was founded on 26 October 1799, and was named after the American president Benjamin Franklin. For most of its 180 years, Franklin was a very quiet city. But then the American Civil War came, and the city was devastated. The Battle of Franklin, which was fought on 30 November 1864, was one of the bloodiest battles of the Civil War. It took a very long time to rebuild the city. Slowly, it was built back up, and today it is one of the wealthiest cities in Tennessee. In fact, it is one of the wealthiest cities in all of the United States.

With its close proximity to Nashville, the centre of the American country–music scene, Franklin attracts a lot of visitors. People living in Franklin have, well, the best of both worlds! The city is a combination of small-town charm and big-city sophistication. If you were to visit Franklin, you could see some cool Civil War sites and museums and gorgeous Victorian homes. Plus, there is tons of shopping. Being a self-described 'shopaholic', you can bet that Miley loves that feature of her hometown!

Probably because Franklin is so close to Nashville, several singers have decided to settle there. Josh Gracin, the fourth-place finisher on the 2003 season of *American Idol 2*, lives in Franklin with his wife and children. Carrie Underwood, *American Idol*'s fourth champ, lives there too. And the pop-punk/emo band Paramore hails from Franklin, as well.

Growing up in Franklin, Miley had an ideal life. She lived there with her big family: mom, dad, older half brothers, Christopher and Trace; older stepsister, Brandi; younger half brother, Braison; and younger half sister, Noah Lindsey. Needless to say, the Cyrus household was one busy place with all those kids running around!

Miley also had lots of pets around. She had three dogs, two cats and seven horses. Braiding her horses' tails was one of Miley's most favourite things to do and something she misses very much since moving to

Los Angeles. After all, you can't keep all those horses in Tinseltown!

Miley's younger years were pretty normal – except for the fact that her dad was a huge country singer! Miley attended Heritage Middle School, a 'regular' school with students and teachers. These days she has a private tutor, since there's no time to commute to a school. Having a private tutor is convenient; the tutor can go wherever you go to give you your lessons. In school, maths and creative writing were among Miley's favourite subjects. She's already put those creative writing lessons to good use, having penned over one hundred songs!

When Miley was in school, she loved to sing and dance. In fact, she had dreams of someday making it to Broadway. So to get some performing experience under her belt, Miley decided to try out for the cheerleading squad and the dance team. In fact, one of Miley's most embarrassing moments happened when she was about to try out for the dance team in primary school. She was wearing a denim skirt that day, and probably because she was so psyched up about the tryouts, she started dancing in the school's hallways. In the middle of a move, Miley slipped – and the skirt ripped! Miley turned bright red. Even though the guidance counsellor was able to fix her skirt, Miley's mom was called, which only added to her embarrassment!

Being the children of Billy Ray meant that the Cyrus clan got a lot of attention, but that was a good training ground for all the attention that was soon to be thrown Miley's way. Not only is Miley following her dad's path to stardom, but so is her little sister, Noah. Born on 8 January 2000, little Noah Lindsey already has a lot on her acting résumé. She has appeared in four episodes of her sister's show, *Hannah Montana.* These episodes are: 'It's a Mannequin's World', where she plays a little shopper; 'O Say, Can You Remember the Words', where she's a little girl on the beach; 'Torn Between Two Hannahs', where again she's a little girl; and 'Money for

Nothing, Guilt for Free', where she plays the role of a little girl in a ball pit who pinches both Lilly (as Lola) and Miley (as Hannah). Noah also appeared in six episodes of her father's television show *Doc*, playing Gracie Herbert.

Billy Ray must be mighty proud of his little girls!

chapter 2
Daddy's Story

Up until now, Billy Ray has always been known for his hit single, 'Achy Breaky Heart', which was not only a catchy tune but was the song that really started the line-dancing craze. But if you ask anyone today under the age of sixteen who Billy Ray Cyrus is, they'd answer: 'Miley's dad!'

Billy Ray was born on 25 August 1961, in Flatwoods, Kentucky, USA. Flatwoods is what you would call a 'bedroom community', meaning that there is no big industry or business in that town. It's what some people call a commuting town – you work in one town and live in another. Flatwoods is a quiet, safe little town, ideal for raising a family.

Interestingly, Flatwoods was not the city's original

name. It was first called Advance, after the Advance Methodist Church. The name was later changed to Cheap, after John Cheap, the Methodist minister – but face it, who would really want to live in a place called *cheap*? In 1938, the city was renamed Flatwoods and has kept the name ever since. Flatwoods is a pretty good name for the place, since there was an area of flat, wooded land that ran through the city. The flat woods were about 650 feet high and ran parallel to the Ohio River.

Billy Ray had a lot of family around him when he was growing up. His paternal grandfather was a Pentecostal preacher. His father, Ronald 'Ron' Ray, sang in the gospel group, the Crownsmen Quartet. Billy Ray's maternal grandmother was a hoedown fiddler, and his mother, Ruth Ann, played bluegrass music. It's easy to see where Billy Ray got his musical talent from.

Billy Ray's parents divorced when he was five years old. Besides being a singer, his father was a popular Democratic politician. In 1975, Ron was elected to the

Kentucky House of Representatives. Ron Cyrus served eleven consecutive terms – a total of twenty-one years. He finally retired from politics in 1996. On 28 February 2006, Ron Cyrus died from lung cancer.

When he was growing up, Billy Ray dreamed of becoming a baseball player. In fact, he attended Georgetown College on a baseball scholarship, fully intending to carry out this dream. But then he bought a guitar and a new chord was struck. Along with his brother Kevin, Billy Ray formed a band called Sly Dog.

Billy Ray loved playing in the band so much that he decided to ditch his baseball-playing dreams. However, he was realistic about the music industry, so he gave himself ten months to find a gig. As luck would have it, one week before his self-imposed deadline, the group got a call to be the house band for a club in Ironton, Ohio. They stayed there for two years, until a fire wiped out the bar – and all of Billy Ray's equipment!

Undaunted, Billy Ray moved to Los Angeles to

pursue his music career. But Billy Ray found that LA was no place for a country singer, so he headed back home. Based in Kentucky, Billy Ray commuted to the place all country crooners try to break into – Nashville! In Nashville, he tried to play gigs, desperately hoping someone would hear him and sign him to a record deal. Someone *did* hear Billy Ray. It was an American country music star named Del Reeves, who introduced Billy Ray to Harold Shedd of Mercury Records. And in the summer of 1990, Billy Ray signed a deal with Mercury.

Within two short years after inking his deal, Billy had a hit. 'Achy Breaky Heart' sold over one million copies and spent five weeks at the top of the Billboard country-music charts – a record that's yet to be broken. (But watch out, Dad, Miley might give you a run for your money someday!) Billy Ray had women swooning at his feet. With his famous 'mullet' haircut – short in the front, long in the back – and a sculpted bod, Billy Ray had to *fend* off the fans with his guitar (well, not literally!).

Even though Billy Ray's first album, *Some Gave All* (from which 'Achy Breaky Heart' was a single), was a mega success, he had a hard time following it up – a *really* hard time. Some say that part of Billy Ray's success was due to his hunky looks and part was due to the catchy tune of 'Achy Breaky Heart'. Whatever the formula, he could never replicate it, and the music world soon forgot poor Billy Ray.

In 1993, Billy Ray came out with the album *It Won't Be the Last*. It hit the charts at number three but fell way short of expectations. When *Storm in the Heartland* came out in 1994, it reached gold but was basically snubbed by the country music stations. And when Billy Ray tried to come back with *Trail of Tears* in 1996, his audience had dwindled even further.

Some people might have been totally devastated by this 'failure', but not Billy Ray. He soon found out that he had another talent – acting. 'I was just kind of doing it as a hobby – just something to do – but I sure wasn't taking it very seriously,' Billy Ray recalled. 'I didn't take it seriously until a few years later when I had a chance to go in and audition for David Lynch's *Mulholland Drive*. David hired me, and it was during the process of filming *Mulholland Drive* that he pulled me to the side and said, "I'm not your agent and not your manager, so I have nothing to gain from this. But I just want to tell you as a director that you could be a very good actor if you want to do that." '

Billy Ray had also been following the careers of two singers, Dolly Parton and Kenny Rogers. He saw that they kept on going even when radio stations were no longer giving their music a lot of airtime. How did they do it? They'd turned to acting.

Taking his cue from his fellow singers, Billy Ray hit the big screen. After filming *Mulholland Drive*, Billy Ray received a script for a TV show called *Doc*. Billy Ray read the script, liked it, auditioned and landed the title role! From 2001 to 2004, Billy Ray played Dr Clint 'Doc'

Cassidy, a Montana doctor who takes a job in a New York medical clinic.

But Billy Ray's love for music never left him. 'Making music comes as naturally to me as taking a breath. It's what I do. Acting is something that I'm constantly trying to learn, every time I take the floor.' In fact, Billy Ray wrote most of his new album, *Wanna Be Your Joe*, which was released 18 July 2006, while filming *Doc*. Billy Ray wrote or co-wrote all the songs on the album, which he describes as 'my most personal album yet'. On the album, Miley joins her dad for one of the tracks – 'Stand'.

Now the reviews are in – and people are loving the new album! Countrystarsonline.com sums up the reviews nicely: 'Forget the mullet. Forget the push and pull of a line-dancing train. Forget the past. Making music with lasting meaning, not for notoriety and not for quick passing chart success, is where this average Joe now finds himself. And there are many who couldn't be happier.' Betcha that Billy Ray's pretty happy too!

Billy Ray thought he'd had enough of acting, and he had returned to music. Then along came *Hannah Montana*.

Miley was cast first in the series, and then they cast her dad. 'This is Miley's thing,' Billy Ray told the *Daily News*. 'She's worked too hard on it, and I didn't want to be responsible for her getting it or not getting it. I didn't want to come in and mess up her show. I've never done comedy and the last thing I want to do is ruin her show.' Don't worry, Dad – you haven't messed things up at all!

But getting the part as Miley's dad on *Hannah Montana* didn't come so easily for Billy Ray. He had to audition – just like everyone else! 'I was as nervous as can be,' Billy Ray told the *New York Daily News*. 'Miley came in and read the scene with me. And then they sent me out and, you know, I sat out in the lobby for a little while. And then they called me back in and I read it again. And then they sent me on my way.'

Of course, Billy Ray got the job. 'They just loved the chemistry between me and my dad,' said Miley. 'It was great, just awesome.' On the show, Billy Ray plays Robbie, Miley's father and manager. The part of Robbie is loosely based on real life. In the show, Robbie is also a famous singer (who doesn't really sing any more . . . sound familiar?). The footage of Robbie as a famous singer is actual footage of Billy Ray himself!

Starring on a Disney Channel show has also brought Billy Ray a whole new slew of fans. A few days after the episode 'I Want My Mullet Back' aired, Billy Ray performed in a concert. 'I looked out and there were all these kids with mullet wigs in the audience,' Billy told OCALA.com. 'They held up signs saying, "Billy, get your mullet back." ' Billy Ray's mullet song, which is on his new CD, is also played at sports arenas, especially during National Hockey League games. Mullet is called 'hockey hair', because a lot of great ice hockey players had mullet dos. These days, Billy Ray is inundated with calls from the

National Hockey League to sing the National Anthem at their games!

'Miley used to be known as Billy Ray Cyrus's daughter,' Billy Ray told the *New York Daily News.* 'Now I'm known as Miley Cyrus's father.'

chapter 3
Stagestruck

Miley was stagestruck at an early age. 'I was singing on the stage with my dad when I was two,' Miley told a reporter. 'I would sing "Hound Dog" and silly songs for the fun of it.'

Although singing corny songs with her dad did not land her a record deal, those early performing days certainly made her feel comfortable singing in front of an audience. This early training helped build Miley into the secure, outgoing, fun girl we all love today. And Miley got a lot of practise writing songs with her dad too. 'Since Miley was a little girl, we've been writing songs together,' Billy Ray told the Associated Press.

But all that singing didn't make Miley into an

immediate pop star. Remember that when Miley was just a tot, her dad was at the top of the charts. But then Billy Ray's star began to slip and he started to act. And guess what? Miley became interested in acting too. Like father, like daughter.

Miley began to get serious about showbiz when she was about nine years old. That was the time when her family moved from Tennessee to Toronto, Canada, where her dad was shooting the television series *Doc*.

Living in Toronto is a far cry from living in Tennessee. First of all, it gets very cold there! Toronto is the largest city in Canada. It's also the capital of the province Ontario. There are about 2.5 million people living in Toronto, making it the fifth most populated city in North America. As you can see, Toronto is much, much larger than Franklin, Tennessee!

But Toronto is a very exciting city in which to live. There's a financial district, with lots of skyscrapers, and residential districts too. There's lots of culture to be had, including theatre, art and music. And, of course, there's lots of shopping!

When Billy Ray won the part of Clint 'Doc' Cassidy in the television series *Doc*, it only made sense to move the family to Toronto, where the show was being filmed. *Doc* is the story of a handsome doctor from rural Montana who takes a job at Westbury Clinic, a small medical centre in the Big Apple – aka New York City. Clint's down-to-earth style and good bedside manner help him win over his patients. However, he faces challenges from other doctors on the staff and the medical system as a whole. Yet Clint manages never to lose his values.

Doc aired on the PAX network from 11 March 2001, through 1 November 2004. The show could be seen in the United States and more than forty other countries around the world. And in one of the shows – episode six of season four – Miley was a guest star. The episode, entitled 'Men in Tights', originally aired on 10 November 2003. In that episode, she played a character named Kylie.

Even though Miley appeared on just one episode of her dad's show, she was hard at work going after her acting dream while they were in Toronto. 'She was quite determined, diligent and persistent,' Billy Ray told a reporter. 'While I was in Toronto, she found the best coaches, worked on her [acting] chops, went to auditions, and did all the different things to reach her goal.' And Miley probably got the feel of what it would be like to be an actor from watching her dad. All those hours she witnessed Dad filming his TV show sure didn't discourage Miley from following her dream.

Also in 2003, Miley appeared on the big screen in Tim Burton's flick *Big Fish*. Although the credits for the film cite her as Destiny Cyrus, it was definitely our Miley in the film! This PG movie is the story about a son trying to learn more about his dying father by reliving stories and myths his father told him about himself. Miley had a very small part in the film – Ruthie, age eight.

When Miley was eleven, she auditioned for a Disney

Channel show. The TV execs were looking for someone who had both acting and singing talent – the best of both worlds! 'We decided we would not go through with this series until we found a kid who could carry a sitcom as well as she could carry a tune,' said Gary Marsh, president of entertainment for Disney Channel Worldwide.

They auditioned a ton of girls who could act as well as Miley, but none of the girls could match her charisma. 'I auditioned forever,' Miley told *USA Today*. 'At first they said I was too small and too young.'

Luckily for Miley – and for us – the network waited for Miley to grow up. And then she landed the biggest part of her life – Hannah Montana!

In Miley, says Gary Marsh, 'we saw a girl who has this natural ebullience. She loves every minute of her life. It shows in her demeanour and performance.'

chapter 4

Disney Days

The Disney Channel has come up with a formula for success – making shows for tweens. If you ask your parents what they thought of when they heard the word *Disney* when they were your age, they'd probably say Mickey Mouse or Donald Duck. Whatever their answer, it probably has something to do with animation.

Disney had to work hard to change this image. They have a great track record at creating stars such as Britney Spears, Justin Timberlake, Keri Russell, and Christina Aguilera. All these stars launched their careers as Mouseketeers in Disney's *Mickey Mouse Club*. And Disney also helped to boost the pop careers of 'N Sync, the Backstreet Boys and Jessica Simpson through their televised concerts. But much to Disney's dismay, these stars really took off outside of the Disney realm. 'We drove these kids into giant success stories,' Disney Channel's Gary Marsh told *Variety*. 'But we thought, "Shouldn't we be growing this internally?" We were making celebrities out of other people's rock stars.' Good thinking, Gary!

In order to grow celebrities, Disney had to come up with the seed from which to grow their stars. In other words, they needed a hook. And that hook ended up being making shows for teens and tweens. *Lizzie McGuire* was Disney's first big catch. 'They just hit that desire button in kids, where they end up personally invested in those programmes,' Terri Minsky, co-creator of *Lizzie McGuire*, told *USA Today*.

Sure, targeting teens and tweens has been part of Disney's secret success, but Disney has added another twist. Take, for example, *That's So Raven*. This is the story of an average teenager, Raven Baxter. She goes through the typical trials and tribulations that every teen goes through – except for one twist – she has psychic powers. Now how cool would it be to have psychic powers? It's a fantasy world that lots of people would love to live. This is another part of Disney's secret – adding an element of wish fulfillment to their stories.

But fantasy aside, the recipe is mostly having characters that today's tweens can relate to – characters that viewers would want to be friends with. 'The bottom line is you know you have good characters when kids go, "Boy, wouldn't it be nice to hang out with them one day," ' Michael Poryes, the executive producer of *Hannah Montana* and *That's So Raven*, told *USA Today*. 'That's the secret, really, to the Disney Channel,' Poryes says. 'We're more about the reality and the truth, what kids really go through: "My friend is going to get dumped by this guy. What am I going to do?" '

Disney has also been hugely successful with its made-for-TV movies like *The Cheetah Girls* and *High School Musical*. These movies combine teen/tween story lines with music. How genius! And the CDs from each of these movies have soared high on the charts.

Now Disney has had hits with *Raven, Lizzie* and *The Suite Life of Zack & Cody*. But Disney wanted more.

Enter *Hannah Montana. Hannah Montana* is the story of fourteen-year-old Miley Stewart, a girl from Tennessee who moves to Malibu, California, with her widowed father, Robbie, and her brother, Jackson. Seems like your average teen story, right? Well, this teen leads a double life as an international singing sensation known as Hannah Montana. How does Miley hide her identity as a pop star? Simple – she wears a blonde wig as Hannah and is her 'regular old self' as Miley. Okay, you have to suspend some disbelief, but it works! Most of the show centres on Miley trying to live her life as an average teen. It's full of laughs, angst and drama – and of course, music! Miley, as Hannah, sings all the songs on the show.

Hannah Montana also has a message: fame is not to be confused with real life. You can only be truly happy when you stay true to yourself. This is a great message – and lesson for tweens to learn.

Let's rewind for a minute. Disney had a great concept, with a great message to boot. But where were they going to get the great star? Gary Marsh did the normal casting calls in LA and in New York, but they didn't find anyone to fit the bill. Marsh was determined to find someone who could act in a sitcom, and sing, plus be what he calls a 'relatable, accessible girl'. Basically they were looking for someone that everyone would want as their friend, but who could sing and act too.

Then one day, a tape came in. It was a tape from an eleven-year-old girl from Tennessee. That tape was from Miley Cyrus. We all know that at this point in her life Miley had no real performing experience, but Miley had that acting bug rooted deep inside her. Miley told *Scholastic News Online* that she knew she wanted to act 'by going to the set with my dad and getting to see the environment and how much fun, joy and encouragement there is on the set. It's great seeing everyone working together as a team on the show. You are all together and you're all in a family, and it's a really great place to be.'

Even though Miley knew she wanted to act and even though Disney thought she was the best one for the job, they were uncomfortable hiring someone with so little actual acting experience. It didn't matter that her dad was a star. It didn't matter that she had raw talent. Disney wanted experience, and that was something Miley could not make up. Luckily, Disney waited.

The execs asked Miley to perform in front of them. She walked into a room of fifteen people, undoubtedly with a big smile on her face and a ton of confidence. And then she sang. That was the first moment it crystallized that she was the 'it' girl.

The producers and network bigwigs loved Miley's acting skills. They felt that she was confident, but not cocky, and her comic timing was near genius. And they were also blown away by her husky-sounding singing voice. 'She has the everyday relatability of Hilary Duff and the stage presence of Shania Twain, and that's an explosive combination,' Gary Marsh told reporters.

Even though the execs were convinced that Miley was the 'it' girl, they still had to sell her to their advertisers and, more importantly, to the viewers. So Disney put on a concert at the Alex Theatre in Glendale, California. The setup was this: a group of seven hundred tweens were invited to a concert and were told that there was a chance to be on TV. A free concert, plus the chance of being on TV – who could refuse?

Miley had only four days to get ready. Feverishly, she worked with a coach and a choreographer to get six songs perfectly staged.

The place was packed. Miley's nerves were probably on edge, her heart racing. But when she hit the stage – as Hannah Montana – the crowd went wild! The reaction surprised everyone, especially Miley! 'It was crazy because I was expecting dead silence,' Miley said. 'They had no idea who Hannah Montana was.'

Disney had sold *Hannah Montana* to the viewers; now it was on to the advertisers. In early spring, television networks unveil their forthcoming series to advertisers. This is called 'upfront'. During the upfronts, TV execs have to convince the advertisers that their show will be a hit. Since advertisers want their commercials to be seen by a lot of people, it only makes sense that they'd want to hook up with a hit show. Lots of viewers equal lots of potential buyers of their products. Most television shows cannot really survive without advertisers. It's all economics. Advertisers pay the networks for their commercial spots; the networks need this money to make a profit. Once the media buyers saw the Hannah Montana 'concert', they were convinced that the show was going to be a hit, and they signed on.

That was a good move. *Hannah Montana* premiered on 24 March 2006 and was an instant hit! Granted, it got a bit of a push by being the lead-in to an encore showing of *High School Musical*, and by having Corbin Bleu (of *High School Musical* fame) guest star on the first episode. But in the end, the episode raked in 5.4 million viewers. Unbelievable! Since then, in its regular time slot in America on Friday evenings, *Hannah Montana* garners over 3.5 million viewers, making it the most popular show among tweens.

Disney's done it again!

chapter 5

Hannah Montana: The Secret Is Out

It would be pretty cool to be a pop star, wouldn't it? Think of all the fame and fortune – the amazing things you could buy with the money you make, the incredible places you'd be able to jet off to. Think of the fans who would follow you around all the time – when you are eating, when you are shopping, when you are trying to relax. You'd have to be nice to your fans; you are obliged to give your autograph. After all, without your fans, you are nothing, right? But it would be nice to have a little quiet time now and then.

The story of *Hannah Montana* is a story that anyone would like to live. 'It's about a rock star who just wants to be with her friends and family and be a normal girl, and she tries to go in disguise and not show everyone she's a rock star because she's supposed to be normal,' Miley told *Time for Kids*. Miley continued describing the show, saying, 'So she goes in disguise and puts on wigs and tons of make-up. At the end she. has her friends, but she also has her secret life of being a rock star.' But *Hannah*'s more than a show about a girl who leads a double life. The show has an underlying theme that lots of teens can relate to – wanting to be someone else, yet working hard to keep your own identity.

In the first episode of *Hannah Montana*, 'Lilly, Do You Want to Know a Secret', Miley Stewart has recently moved from rural Tennessee to snazzy Malibu, California. Miley Stewart is your typical fourteen-year-old kid, with a best friend named Lilly. Everyone their age is just wild about pop star Hannah Montana, and they are all bummed when Hannah's concert is sold out. Then, Lilly scores two tickets and she invites Miley to come along. The only problem is that Miley is really Hannah Montana. How can she be onstage and in the audience at the same time? Miley really doesn't want to spill her secret to Lilly, because she's afraid her friend won't treat her the same any more. Miley loves the relationship they have now, but she's scared that if Lilly finds out her true identity, she'll treat her like a pop star and stop being the true friend she is. This is a dilemma that lots of teens can relate to. They want their friends to like them for who they are inside; they don't want them to like them, say, because their family has a lot of money, or they have a famous relative, or because of how they dress.

But when Lilly sneaks into Hannah's dressing room, she eventually discovers that Miley is really Hannah Montana. What a shock that is to Lilly! Lilly is really upset that Miley didn't tell her the truth – after all, they are best friends, and best friends are supposed to tell each other everything, right? In the end, though, Lilly and Miley make up, and Lilly agrees to keep Miley's secret.

Keeping secrets is something everyone can relate to. They are sometimes hard to keep, and we're always scared that somehow our secrets are going to leak out. Having – and keeping – secrets is part of growing up. There are secrets about who you have a crush on and secrets about whom your best friends have a crush on. There are secrets about presents you are buying and secrets about presents others are buying for you.

Some people are great at keeping secrets. Other people are, well, not so great at it. Miley Stewart and Hannah Montana are great at keeping secrets, but Miley Cyrus? Not so much. When asked about how the real-life Miley resembles the TV Miley, Miley told *Discovery Girls* magazine: 'The differences are easiest – I'm not very good at keeping secrets at all! If you want your secret kept, don't tell me! I'll be triggered by a memory and I'll just want to say what it is! Or I'll say to my mom, "You will not believe what is happening!" '

But it's no secret that *Hannah Montana* has been a huge hit. The debut show drew Disney's highest audience ever for an original series. In fact in the 2006 season, among kids ages two to eleven, *Hannah* was right behind *American Idol* as the most-watched show.

Even though Miley loves working on the show, it's a lot of hard work. Not only does she have to put in long hours on the set, but she has to play two different parts! 'To be able to stay in there and focused is the best thing you got to do,' Miley told *KnoxNews*.

One of Miley's favourite moments in the first season of the show was getting to work with country music star Dolly Parton. Miley has known Dolly for many years, but just as a friend of her dad's. (The two had performed together on several occasions.) But now Miley was getting to work with her on a professional basis, and she was psyched! In the episode 'Good Golly, Miss Dolly', Dolly Parton plays the part of Miley's aunt. Aunt Dolly gives Miley lots of advice about her love life and almost messes things up between Miley and her crush, Jake Ryan. Miley, who calls Dolly 'Aunt Dolly' in real life, must have been very comfortable with this role on the show.

A thing like almost having your secret crush revealed is something that a lot of girls can relate to. In fact, most of the *Hannah Montana* episodes offer very valuable life lessons. Betcha that you've come across some of these situations in your life:

Unrequited love: In 'Miley Get Your Gum', Miley's friend Oliver has a crush on Hannah Montana. Of course, Hannah does not feel the same way. Miley and Lilly try to talk him out of his crush, but no deal. So, Miley 'fesses up that she's really Hannah Montana. Crush over.

Disobeying your parents: In 'She's a Supersneak', Miley and Jackson desperately want to meet Ashton Kutcher at his movie premiere. But Dad says they can't go. Not wanting to miss this opportunity, Miley and Jackson sneak out, only to later get caught red-handed by Dad!

Lying to your best bud: In 'It's My Party, and I'll

Lie if I Want To', Miley lies to Lilly about going to a party. But when the paparazzi nab Hannah Montana at the bash, Lilly finds out. Of course she's hurt, but in the end, the true friends make up.

Trying to play matchmaker: In 'Oops! I Meddled Again', Miley and Lilly try to set Oliver up with a girl at school named Becca. But this is no easy setup, and things get more complicated as the girls meddle further into the lovebirds' business.

Being vain: In 'You're So Vain, You Probably Think This Zit Is About You', Lilly has to wear glasses right before a big skateboarding competition, and Miley gets a big zit that shows up on her poster picture.

Forgetting that your best friend is more important than your crush: In 'More Than a Zombie to Me', Miley turns down Jake Ryan's offer to go to the dance. But when Miley finds out that Lilly agreed to go with Jake, she decides to try to steal Jake away. She ends up really hurting Lilly, but eventually realizes that no boy should come between a girl and her best bud.

When Miley goes out in public, sometimes her fans are confused. They don't know whether to call her Miley or Hannah. After all, she is both girls, right? Well, sort of. The real person here is Miley Cyrus. Hannah Montana is fictional. Yet, when Miley tours, she is Hannah, so she really doesn't mind when her fans call her that. Miley figures that fans probably call her by the name of the character they feel most comfortable with, or who they can relate to the best. If they like the sparkly, outgoing, performing type, then they call her Hannah. It they relate better to the girl-next-door type, the girl who just wants to fit in, then they call her Miley.

Sometimes, life can get a bit confusing for Miley. But one thing's for sure – she's a star!

chapter 6

Living the Life

When MediaVillage asked Miley Cyrus if she thought *Hannah Montana* was going to become really popular, Miley said, 'I hope so. Hannah in the show is enormous, like a Hilary Duff of TV. I hope everyone really likes her. She's a great person.'

Well, Miley's 'hope' certainly has come true. *Hannah Montana* is an enormous success. But how has life changed for Miley since becoming a mega star? Well, it's changed in lots of ways.

First of all, Miley and her family now live in Los Angeles. 'Everything is completely different,' Miley told *Discovery Girls* magazine. 'I come from this really small town near Nashville, Tennessee, where everything was la-di-da and normal. And then, all of a sudden, everything is completely the opposite. I went from living in slow motion to living at two hundred miles an hour!'

You can say that again. LA is a far cry from Miley's hometown of Franklin, Tennessee. And even though Miley had a taste of city life when she lived in Toronto, nothing compares to LA.

Los Angeles is the most populated city in the state of California – there are thirteen million people living there! LA is the home to major cultural centres, science and technology industries, and, of course, it is the place where movies, TV shows and music are made.

When Miley moved to LA and began the gruelling schedule of filming a TV show, she had to give up going to public school. She now spends about three hours a day with a tutor in order to keep up with her studies.

Miley got a big clue that her life had changed when her little sister, Noah, told her that she had entered a contest on the Disney Channel website to win backstage passes to a concert featuring the network's newest star –

Miley Cyrus. 'You live with me!' Miley told her sister. And then, according to *The New York Times*, Miley warned her sister not to swipe anything from her room to sell on eBay!

A Miley Cyrus possession would probably go for big bucks on eBay. These days, fans are going wild just at the sight of her. 'The last time me and my mom went [shopping], it turned out not to be such a good idea,' Miley told MSNBC.com. 'People rushed into the store we were in, and they had to shut the doors until everyone would go away. It was crazy.'

Crazy, but true. Miley is now a *huge* star. But even though she's super popular now, Miley hasn't lost her down-to-earth charm or her Tennessean drawl. She's always greeting people with a 'How y'all doing?' Miley is the kind of girl you'd love to have for a friend. She's loyal and honest and a lot of fun to be around. In fact, she's a lot like the character Miley Stewart she plays on TV.

When *Scholastic News Online* asked Miley to

describe Miley and Hannah, here's what she had to say: 'Miley is just like me, but she's also like any other average girl going through love stuff, friend stuff and family stuff. But she is trying to get through the pressure of being a universal superstar. Everyone loves Hannah, but she just wants to have her friends and her family.'

Fans may idolize Hannah, but Miley has a few idols of her own. Beyoncé, the soulful lead singer of Destiny's Child and smokin' solo artist, is one of Miley's idols. Miley would love to have a career as amazing as Beyoncé's (and she likes her fashion sense too!). Another star that Miley looks up to is Raven, the star of Disney Channel's *That's So Raven*. Miley thinks Raven is a loving person – and totally funny too!

Miley's also a big Hilary Duff fan. In fact, Miley's entire family loves Hilary! Miley thinks that it's very cool that Hilary started *Lizzie McGuire* at the same age Miley started *Hannah Montana*. 'The way that I am doing the business and everything is kind of following in her

Miley Cyrus

Miley greeting fans at a VH1 event

Miley signing
autographs at a
movie premiere

Miley and her
dad, country
music star
Billy Ray Cyrus

Miley posing with Mitchel Musso, who plays Oliver on *Hannah Montana*

Miley and Emily Osment get friendly on the red carpet. Emily plays Lilly on *Hannah Montana*.

Miley sings her heart out as Hannah Montana.

footsteps,' Miley told a reporter on the set of her show. 'So watching her grow as a singer and an actress is helping me as well.'

If you think about it, Miley Cyrus's life kind of mirrors the life of the character she plays on TV. Miley Cyrus is trying to get through the pressures of being a big star, yet she's still an average girl at heart. Miley still has to do things at home, like clean her room and make her bed. And, like lots of teens, she sometimes gets in trouble for talking back to her parents. 'When I get home I'm really not in the mood to deal with my brother or little sister, and so usually I'm kind of snapping at them,' Miley told *Popstar!* magazine. And like a true teen, Miley insists that her behaviour is not her fault – her siblings started it!

Miley really just wants to be treated like the girl next door. She doesn't want fans to be afraid of her because she's a star. Miley, as Miley Cyrus the actress, doesn't have an alter ego to hide behind. All she has is her honesty and modesty to show to fans. 'I wouldn't want to be treated differently,' Miley told *Girls' Life Magazine*. 'I wouldn't want to be someone you couldn't say hello to. I want to be very approachable. Say "hi" to me. I love it.' Miley wants all her fans to have a chance to take a picture with her or to have an autograph signed. So, the next time you see Miley, make sure you say hello!

However, when Miley goes out now, she can't enjoy the same relative anonymity that she enjoyed a few years ago. Today, when Miley hits the streets, she's recognized instantly. There are no more quiet shopping jaunts or relaxing trips to the movies for Miley. Once, she went to the Universal Studios theme park with her brother and a friend, and she was immediately recognized. 'It was craziness,' Miley told a reporter. 'All the kids on every ride. I felt like I was going to hurl after one ride, and all the kids were like, "Hannah Montana is about to puke!" ' One thing is for sure: when you're a star, you have to be ready to sacrifice all sense of privacy.

Even though Miley's constantly stalked by frenetic

fans, she gets nervous when she meets one of her idols. Once, when she met Judge Judy, Miley freaked! 'She's my idol! I was like, "Oh my goodness, what do I say to her? I'm so nervous! What if she thinks I'm so weird?"' But Judge Judy was perfectly nice to Miley and made her feel comfortable. After that encounter, Miley *really* knows how her fans feel when they meet her.

Still, it's hard to deal with all those fans. Sure, most fans are psyched to meet Miley and would do anything for an autograph or a photo op. But there are others who are, well, downright rude. Miley told *Discovery Girls* magazine about a funny run-in she had with a fan: 'I was having lunch with my brother and I had on my pyjamas. I wasn't wearing make-up, and my hair was totally nasty. So we get to the restaurant and the first thing I hear is, "You look a lot better on TV." Sometimes it's really weird to hear stuff like that. I just think, "Well, that was harsh!" But then again there are times when someone will come up to me and say, "Omigosh! You're so cute and I love your shoes." And when that happens I just think, "This is sweet!" '

Yes, life is certainly turning out to be very sweet for Miley Cyrus.

chapter 7

Make New Friends, but Keep the Old

Miley's move to LA brought mixed emotions. Sure, she was totally thrilled to land the role as Hannah Montana, but getting that part meant that she and her family would have to move. When Billy Ray landed the part in *Doc*, the family's move to Toronto was more temporary. This move looked like it was going to be for real.

Moving to LA meant saying good-bye to her farm, to her animals, to her grandparents and to her best buds. 'It was bittersweet,' Miley told *J-14* magazine. 'I hung out with a small group of friends I've known all my life because I went to the same school my whole life.'

Miley was especially going to miss her best friend, Lesley. Miley and Lesley had known each other since they were six years old. The pair did everything together. 'I was used to seeing her every day and talking to her all the time,' Miley told *J-14*. 'Once I moved to LA, I knew I wasn't going to see her at all.' Lesley was a true friend to Miley – through and through! When Miley was going through the gruelling audition process at Disney, Lesley was there to offer encouragement. When Miley was bummed about moving to LA, Lesley was there to cheer her up.

Right before the big move, the best buds had one last day together. The girls couldn't stop bawling at the thought of being separated. When Miley's mom came to pick her up, Miley told her that she didn't want to leave. Miley's mom was supportive and told her that she didn't have to make the big move if she didn't want to. But deep down inside, Miley knew that she had to go; if she didn't, she'd be giving up her dream of becoming a star.

Even though Miley lives two thousand miles away from her friends in Tennessee, she has managed to keep in touch with them – especially Lesley. In fact, Lesley made it out to LA to catch Miley's first big concert. Miley was really glad that Lesley was there with her for her first gig. Having her best bud around sure helped calm Miley's nerves. And Lesley continues to visit Miley lots. 'I realize now that you can't be afraid to lose people,' Miley told *J-14* magazine, 'and that's the thing I was afraid of the most. You can't lose somebody if you always hold on to them.'

Moving is hard for anyone. You have to get used to a new city or town and a new house. You have to get used to a new school. But the hardest thing to do when you move is to make new friends. This is especially difficult when you are in middle school. By this time, most kids have already found their groups and breaking into a new clique can be next to impossible.

But Miley was lucky. Sure, she had to get used to an entirely new city and house, but since she was going to be working 24/7, she wouldn't be going to a normal school, so she wouldn't have to deal with the social pressures there. Also, Miley's not the type of kid to shrink into a corner and not talk to anyone new. Just the opposite – Miley's bubbly personality made it easy for her to fall in with the Hollywood set.

Miley has made a lot of new friends in Hollywood. One of her new buds is Ashley Tisdale. Miley even has a picture of them on the screen saver of her Sidekick phone. Some people have said that when Miley dons her blonde wig, the two can pass for sisters!

Miley has also been lucky to make friends on her show. She's become very tight with Emily Osment, who plays Lilly Truscott, and Mitchel Musso, who plays Oliver Oken. Miley has also become close with Jason Daniel Earles, who plays her older brother, Jackson.

In real life, Jason was born on 26 April in San Diego, California. The exact year of his birth is somewhat of a mystery. Some reports say 1985, while others list 1977. That's an eight-year difference, and Jason's keeping mum about the truth! Jason can be seen in the movie *National*

Treasure, and he worked on *Phil of the Future*, playing the role of Grady Spaggett, an advanced maths student.

When Jason first started working on *Hannah Montana*, he couldn't believe how well everyone got along. 'This group got really tight, really quickly', Jason told *Popstar!* magazine. '. . . By the end of the pilot, all the kids were like swapping numbers and staying over each other's houses and hanging out'. Jason says that they all became so close, they started acting like a real family – complete with bickering. But no worries – they always made up!

Even though Miley is cool with her onscreen brother, offscreen she hangs out more with Emily and Mitchel. Co-star Emily Osment plays Lilly Truscott, Hannah Montana's (and Miley Stewart's) best friend. Emily Jordan Osment is a California girl. She was born in Los Angeles on 10 March 1992. Living in the land of the stars, acting was in the air. It was also in her blood. Her dad, Eugene Osment, is an actor, as is her older brother, Haley Joel Osment (of *The Sixth Sense* fame).

When Emily was five years old, her dad asked her if she wanted to get into the biz. Eager to break in (or as eager as any five-year-old could be!), Emily started doing commercials, and in 1999, she landed her first film, *The Secret Life of Girls*. Following this, Emily appeared in Hallmark's *Sarah, Plain and Tall: Winter's End*. Other TV work included *3rd Rock from the Sun*, *Touched by an Angel* and *Friends*. Then in 2002, she landed the role of Gerti Giggles in *Spy Kids 2: Island of Lost Dreams*. When writer/director Robert Rodriguez saw Emily audition, he was so blown away that he wanted to give her more screen time, so made her role in the film longer! Emily then went on to star in *Spy Kids 3D: Game Over*.

With such an impressive résumé, you'd think that Emily would have had no problem landing the part of Lilly. There's no way she'd have to wait as long as Miley did for her part. Well, the role didn't come so easily to her. She had to audition about three or four times. At her last audition, when Miley was already cast, they had Emily read with Miley. The two obviously had some chemistry, and Emily won the part!

Emily admits that she had no idea that *Hannah Montana* would become such a hit. When she first landed the part, she thought she was going to be part of a cute show, something that would quietly air on Disney. Even after they shot the pilot and people were gushing at how great it was, Emily was not fazed. Boy, was she surprised at the way things turned out!

When Emily first started filming *Hannah Montana*, she would have never guessed that she'd soon be recognized by fans as soon as she stepped out her door. True, when the show first hit, people would approach her and ask if she played Lilly, but now when fans see her, there's no doubt in their minds who she is!

When TheStarScoop.com asked Emily how she and Lilly were alike and different, here's what she had to say: 'I think I'm most like Lilly because I really like to do sports. She's a really sporty girl. She likes to get on her skateboard . . . She's really out there and social, and that's sort of like me too. And I think the way I'm sort of not like Lilly, is, she has . . . the coolest clothes I have ever seen . . . I would love to have those kind of clothes.'

Both Emily and Miley like to shop. Emily told *Popstar!* magazine that she likes to shop at lots of stores, like Abercrombie and Old Navy. But she's always on the prowl for one-of-a-kind clothes and accessories. 'I really like little boutiques. I like stuff that I'll wear and people will go, "Oh, where'd you get that?" They have no idea where I got it. I love that.' And Miley is a self-admitted 'shopaholic'. And her shopping 'habit' has got worse since she's moved to LA. 'I'm a big shoe person,' Miley told *USA Today*. 'Sometimes I'll be punky, the next day I'll be preppy.'

Even though Lilly and Miley are best buds on screen, in real life, they are complete opposites! Emily's really into soccer. She's been playing since she's been six years old. 'It's so much fun and my whole family's in on it,' Emily told *Popstar!* magazine. 'We all go to soccer games.'

Miley's favourite sport is cheerleading. Growing up, Miley loved to dance and she figured what better way to show her moves than by being a cheerleader? So that's just what she did when she was a student back in Tennessee. Miley's bubbly personality sure makes her the perfect cheerleader type. But since Miley's so busy filming and recording these days, she really doesn't have to be on a team. Although, you can bet that she's always cheering her co-stars on!

As with all friends, Miley and Emily don't agree on everything. But the two are always trying hard to make their friendship work. Miley told *Discovery Girls* magazine that when she and her friends fight, 'I try to be the bigger person. There's no harm in saying "You know what? Whatever. I'm going to let it roll off." '

On the set, Miley and Emily have a blast acting together, but they also have fun as pranksters. 'Emily and

I always get into trouble and pull pranks on each other,' Miley told *J-14* magazine.

Miley is also tight with her other co-star, Mitchel Musso. Mitchel plays Oliver, Miley's other best friend. Besides Lilly, Oliver is Miley's only other friend who knows about her dual identities.

Mitchel had a harder time than his co-stars breaking into the biz. After landing his first commercial gig pretty easily, Mitchel thought showbiz was a breeze. Then came a line of rejections. But Mitchel stuck with it and persevered.

Mitchel had a role in the movie *Secondhand Lions* – along with his younger brother Marc and Emily Osment's brother Haley Joel Osment. And by the time Mitchel auditioned for *Hannah Montana*, he already had a Disney Channel movie under his belt – he starred as Kyle Massey's asthmatic best friend Raymond Figg in *Life Is Ruff*.

But, like his co-stars, his role on *Hannah Montana* didn't come easily. Of course, he had to audition, and during it, he didn't exactly follow the script. Instead of climbing through a window using a chair to stand on, Mitchel used the desk that the execs, who were auditioning him, were sitting at! That was a pretty bold move, but the improvising helped to land him the part.

Both on and off screen, Miley, Mitchel and Emily are tight. They are like one big happy family! The threesome could be spotted at the mall together after taping has wrapped for the day, and when they get home, they three-way call one another at night. Miley may have had to uproot herself from Tennessee to move to LA, but she has certainly found friends who make her feel right at home!

Speaking of friends, what about boys? As in boyfriends? Even though Miley's allowed to date, there's no one out there who has stolen her heart – yet. Sure she has some celeb crushes like American music star Ryan Cabrera, but she's way too busy to start dating. But that's not to say she doesn't have opinions about the opposite sex. One thing she can't stand are cocky boys – the ones who are full of 'tude, and of themselves! Miley's skin crawls when she sees dudes who can't take their eyes off themselves in the mirror. Miley also can't figure out the competitive streak that runs through some boys. For them, winning is everything; Miley just wants to have fun.

This is not to say that Miley's anti-boy. What's her ideal crush? A guy who can make her laugh! Of course, lots of boys can probably do this; Miley's just waiting for the perfect one to come along.

chapter 8

Daddy's Little Girl (and Mom's Too)

Imagine getting the job of a lifetime and then finding out that your dad will be working right alongside you. Talk about cramping your style! But bubbly Miley has never let this get her down. She loves working with her dad. 'It's kind of cool,' she told MediaVillage.com. 'But like with anybody, it's kind of weird at the same time. But it's really good to have him there when he can support me. If I ever have a question, my dad's right there!'

And in an interview with *Discovery Girls* magazine, Miley said this about working with her dad: 'It's weird because at home, I'm a normal . . . girl. I'll say, "Dad, you are so annoying! Leave me alone!" ' Then, Miley says on the long drive from their home to the set, her dad makes her talk about what was bothering her. And Miley has no option but to 'fess up, since he has a captive audience! (She can't get out of the car while they're speeding down the freeway, can she?)

But Miley and Billy Ray make sure that they don't take their work home with them. They don't even practise their lines together at home. 'Anything that happens on the set, stays on the set,' Miley explained. When they are at home, they act just like a real family, not a created-for-TV family. Miley wants Billy Ray to be her *dad* at home, not her *co-worker*.

When Billy Ray was offered the role of Robbie Stewart, he didn't immediately jump at the chance. He was so proud that Miley got the part, and he didn't want to come on the show and mess things up for her. Even though Billy Ray had a pretty successful run with his show *Doc*, he also had his share of letdowns and failures. After all these years, he was still mostly known for 'Achy Breaky Heart'. All of his follow-up releases were a disappointment, at least commercially. Perhaps Billy Ray didn't want to carry that stigma with him to Miley's show. However, Billy Ray is now glad he signed on for the show and he's mighty proud of his little girl too. 'I don't mean to sound like too much of a proud papa,' Billy Ray told the *Daily News*, 'but she is just amazing. I've seen that child go to so many auditions and be turned away and just keep on keeping on.'

Still, when you are teenager, there are times when you just don't want your dad around. Since Miley's on the set a lot, and since she's close with her co-stars, she's probably had some personal conversations with them. You know, the kind of conversations that are definitely *not* for Dad's ears. You could be gossiping with your friends, planning a shopping spree, dishing about your crush, or talking about some hot party. Although Miley says that her dad is 'cool', one can't help but think that there are some times when she just wants her space.

Billy Ray has been careful about giving Miley breathing room. When filming the show, he'd never give

Miley acting tips. In fact, Miley would be more likely to show her dad what to do!

Even though Billy Ray is not hovering over Miley every second of the day, he can sometimes be pretty embarrassing to have around. One day, one of the prop guys on the set gave Billy Ray a farting machine. Every time Miley walked by, Billy Ray made the machine go off. He did this during the filming of her scenes too. And, of course, when the fart was heard, Billy Ray would immediately blame Miley as the one who dealt it. How embarrassing!

Even off the set Dad doesn't let up. One time Miley saw Kelly Clarkson at an event, and Billy Ray went right up to her and told her that Miley was her biggest fan. And then he asked Kelly if Miley could take a picture with her. Come on, Dad, give Miley a break!

Miley told MediaVillage.com that her dad can embarrass her during photo shoots too. 'He'll just yell out things I wouldn't want anyone to know. Just random stuff.

"Remember that time when you were a kid?" That kind of stuff.' But Dad's antics don't make Miley angry. She knows he's just joking around in order to break the ice. Plus it puts a smile on everyone's face – even Miley's!

But joking aside, Billy Ray can be pretty protective of his little girl. When Miley first wanted to enter the business, her dad cautioned her against it. He warned her that Hollywood could be a nasty place. And when she was auditioning like crazy, Billy Ray told her to take some time off. He was worried that she was too focused on becoming a star. He wanted her to take time to enjoy the 'regular' things in her life, like cheerleading and riding horses. But Miley would hear none of this. She was persistent and pressed on. Her serious attitude certainly impressed her dad. Billy Ray told the *New York Daily News*, 'I'm very proud of her that she would set a goal and not stop.'

Billy Ray has been a good role model for Miley. He has taught her to never stop chasing her dream.

In an interview before the 2006 CMA (Country Music Association) Awards, Miley was asked what her dad's best advice has been, and Miley said that it was to just be happy and to love what she's doing. But Miley also said that Billy Ray has told her, 'No matter what you do, don't listen to me, listen to your mom!'

Miley's mom, Tish, is her manager, so you can bet that Miley listens to her! Miley says that her mom is stricter than her dad. Billy Ray admits that he's never been good with discipline. What he tries to do, he told *USA Today*, is to 'use psychology, make 'em laugh or tell a story to make a point'.

Even though Tish is more of the disciplinarian, it doesn't mean that mother and daughter don't have time for fun. 'Every day after work my mom and I go shopping,' Miley told *USA Today*. And when Billy Ray doesn't want to buy something, Mom's always there with a good reason why it's a must.

Besides filming *Hannah Montana* together, Billy

Ray and Miley have travelled around the country making appearances and presentations together. At the 2006 World Series in St Louis, Missouri, Miley and Billy Ray performed the National Anthem together. The pair were scheduled to sing at the Major League Baseball game on Wednesday night, but they were rained out. When they finally did get to sing, Billy Ray was mighty proud. 'It's a feeling of going full circle,' Billy Ray told OCALA. com. 'To look at my little girl standing there, and have the chance to sing together at the World Series is very special. I sing the National Anthem a lot, but I never sang it as a duet with my daughter.'

The father-daughter team also presented at the 40th Annual CMA Awards in November 2006. This was the first year that the awards were back in Nashville after a brief run in New York City. Miley must have been excited to be back in her home state! When Miley and Billy Ray hit the podium to present their award, she told him to take off his sunglasses. Billy retorted by saying, 'I don't tell you what to wear.' Miley's comeback? 'That's right. Remember the mullet.'

And the two presented at the American Music Awards on 21 November 2006. Plus, they hosted the National Celebration of the Boys & Girls Club, which was held in LA on 16 September 2006.

With all those appearances, Billy Ray and Miley sure spend a lot of time together. Billy Ray knows that on top of being Miley's father, he also has to be her friend. Just like the characters they play on TV, Billy Ray lets Miley know that whatever she wants to talk about, he's there for her.

'Miley and I have a great relationship,' Billy Ray said in a Boys & Girls Club interview. 'I think it's important as parents and neighbours that we spend quality time with children and to encourage others in our community to do the same.'

To that, Miley added, 'My dad and I talk all the time about the important stuff in my life. He and my mom know how much I appreciate them, and our relationship is good because we spend time together.'

Miley may be a big star now, but to her parents, she's still their little girl!

chapter 9
The Achy Breaky Charts

Miley loves both her parents, but she's really Daddy's girl. At least, that's whose footsteps she's been following.

In 1992, Billy Ray was at the top of the charts with his 'Achy Breaky Heart'. His album *Some Gave All* spent a whopping seventeen weeks at the top of the Billboard 200 and sold a whopping nine million copies, making it a verified chart buster.

But along came Miley. On 24 October 2006, the *Hannah Montana* CD was released and immediately catapulted to number one on the Billboard Top 200 chart. In its first week, the album sold an unbelievable 281,000 copies.

It's true that Miley's amazing voice has contributed

to the album's success, but there's something else at work here – Disney. Just like it has done with its TV shows, Disney has done a genius job marketing music to the tween set. In the '90s, Disney sold millions of its soundtracks to movies like *The Lion King* and *The Little Mermaid*. But as we said before, Disney-made stars like Christina Aguilera and Justin Timberlake didn't release their music with Disney.

Today, Disney is singing a different song. The *High School Musical* soundtrack has sold well over three million copies. *High School Musical* made it to the number one spot twice, and was the number one bestselling album of '06 in America. And the soundtrack to *The Cheetah Girls 2* debuted in the number five slot on the Billboard Top 200 album chart in August 2006.

Disney has certainly figured out what today's tweens want. But what do these new stars have that has made them so successful? Well, first of all, they all have talent. But, they are also young, have positive messages in their songs, and a lot of them are girls. In the last few years, magazines like *BOP* and *Tiger Beat* have been plastering female pop stars on their covers. 'What these girls are doing is a milestone for pop music,' Leesa Coble, editor-in-chief of *BOP* and *Tiger Beat*, told the *Milwaukee Journal Sentinel*. 'In the past it was all about the guys . . . Cute boys are still really important, but now you're seeing all these female faces too.'

Another thing these new pop stars have going for them is that they get your parents' stamp of approval. No racy lyrics here. No questionable issues are being sung about. Songs from artists like Miley and the Cheetah Girls are good, clean fun. And they are catchy too!

In the summer of 2006, Miley toured with the Cheetah Girls, performing as their opening act. At each of these shows, you could find thousands of young girls – mostly with their mothers – cheering in the stands. And when Miley – dressed as Hannah Montana – went onstage, the fans went wild! Remember: these shows were billed as Cheetah Girls concerts, but Miley's fans were there en masse.

'I'm Hannah Montana! Let's get this party started! How y'all doing tonight!' is what Miley says when she takes the stage at a Cheetah Girls concert. The crowd roars back. They are psyched that Miley/Hannah is the warm-up act for the Girls. When Miley sings, the audience sings along with her – and so do most of the moms!

At each of the Cheetah Girls concerts, Miley could be counted on to belt out her beautiful melodies, with lyrics that speak to the tweens and teens in the audience. When you listen to Miley's lyrics, you feel as though she understands all the stuff you're going through in your life.

When Miley is performing, she feels great. 'As soon as I step on that stage, nothing matters. I don't think of it as work. It's just so much fun,' she said. And it's true, when you watch Miley sing – even when she's dressed like Hannah Montana – it does not look for one minute that she's out onstage because it's a job. This girl truly loves to perform.

But giving a good performance is not as easy as you may think. Sure, Miley has an awesome voice and a personality made to win over any audience, but there's a lot that goes into prepping for a show. Every move that Miley makes on the stage is choreographed. That means hours upon hours of working with a choreographer or dance instructor. Besides working with a choreographer, Miley has backup dancers that she has to learn the routines with. All this coordination means lots of rehearsal time. Not only does Miley have to spend time working with the dancers, but she has to go on the road with them, too. Luckily, Miley's sunny personality has enabled her to make fast friends with her crew. And when she steps out on the stage to sing the songs from her CD, she's super-confident.

The *Hannah Montana* soundtrack features eight songs performed by Miley (as Hannah), including 'The

Best of Both Worlds', 'Who Said', 'Just Like You', 'Pumpin'
Up the Party', 'If We Were a Movie', 'I Got Nerve', 'The
Other Side of Me' and 'This Is the Life'. She also performs
a duet with her dad – 'The Other Side of Me'. Jesse
McCartney, the Click Five, Everlife and B5 contribute to
the other tracks.

Miley loves to write songs, too. 'It's something
that comes naturally,' she told *Scholastic News Online*.
'. . . it's not a step-by-step thing where I sit down and
start writing and singing a tune in my head. Sometimes,
I will just hear it and have something stuck with me all
day and I will go write about that. Or, maybe I will take
something someone said and turn it into a song.'

Miley's music has won over her audience by being
smart, catchy and cool. Being cool and family friendly is
not easy to pull off, but Miley has certainly done it!

chapter 10

Backstage Pass

Even though Miley is the star of her TV show, she still has to share a dressing room with her dad! But Miley's not obsessed about her privacy. In fact, it's just the opposite! 'My room's like the party room,' Miley told *BOP* magazine. 'The radio's always on and the music's blasting. No one knocks – they just fling open the door and get ready to party!'

Once, when they were having a party, Emily Osment thought it would be funny if Miley tripped in front of everyone. (Emily's a big practical joker.) So Emily stuck out her foot, and Miley went flying! Was Miley angry? No, she cracked up!

Mitchel Musso loves hanging out in the Cyruses' dressing room too. Sometimes he'll eat lunch in there and afterwards Billy Ray gives him guitar lessons.

With the music blasting, Miley is always dancing. It's probably a good way to release some of the tension that has built up over the long day of filming. Miley loves to teach Emily Osment new dances. The two girls pump up the volume and rock out!

If you were to look on the walls of Miley's dressing room, you'd see lots of posters, including one of Kelly Clarkson. Kelly is one of Miley's idols. Some people have told Miley that the two look alike! Miley thinks that Kelly is an amazing singer and performer. In fact, Kelly has inspired Miley to hit the stage. Miley loves Kelly's cool style and would love to have a career as awesome as hers.

Besides a poster of her idol, you could see a poster of hottie Orlando Bloom as well as the mega-talented actress Keira Knightley. Miley also likes to clip cool ads from magazines and plaster them on the walls, like one of the hugest diamond ring she ever saw!

Also hanging on the wall of Miley's dressing room

is a collage that her best friend Lesley (from Tennessee) made her. It has about forty pictures on it, including shots of the girls wearing cool shades, dressed in their finest, and making silly faces. Also in the collage is a photo of Miley's cheerleading squad. Another collage that's on the wall has pictures of the Olsen twins, Beyoncé and Orlando Bloom.

Even though Miley shares her dressing room with her dad, you can tell that she's the decorator. Besides all the posters and collages on the wall, there is other stuff in there that is clearly Miley's, like the pink pillows, the pink candles, the pink picture frames and a cheetah-print chair that's shaped like a big shoe!

When Miley's on the road, she always rides in style! Miley used to ride around in a tour *van*. Now, she's been upgraded to a tour *bus*. And it's no wonder – when Miley's on the road she needs lots of clothes, both for herself and her alter ego, Hannah. And don't forget the wig!

Miley loves travelling on her tour bus. And who

wouldn't when you're riding in style! Miley has her own bunk, complete with a TV. When she needs to chill, she just hops on her bed and pops in a movie. And when she's tired, she cuddles under her Elvis blanket and takes a nap!

Miley also never hits the road without her supercool Sidekick phone. Come on, how else could she keep in touch with her friends?

Miley's tour bus has sure done a lot of miles. And her fans are always waiting for her. At Miley's concert debut in Los Angeles, her set opened with the lights down. There was a slow build to her entrance – first there was video of her in her dressing room, and then the audience saw footage of her walking toward the stage. The crowd was wild with anticipation. But wait – there was a glitch! The lights suddenly came back on. A stage manager told the audience they were experiencing some technical difficulties. As the minutes ticked by, the audience waited patiently. Then, the whole thing started over again – dressing room and all. But no one seemed to mind.

Miley never lets her fans down. At a record signing in New York City, two thousand fans were lined up, all eager to get her autograph. Some stars have a time limit for their signings. After an hour, they're out of there! But not Miley – she stayed until the last autograph was penned. Miley was probably beat after all that signing – not to mention the fact that her hand probably ached – but all she could think about was her fans. She was totally amazed at how patient they all were waiting for *her*.

When Miley hits the stage, her fans go absolutely wild. 'It's totally crazy,' Miley told a reporter for Tommy2 .net. 'After a while you kinda forget. On my first couple [of] concerts, the whole time it kinda threw me off. But they just forget about that because they do a really good job of helping you sing along.'

Miley admits that she sometimes gets nervous

before a show. She told *Popstar!* magazine that before her *Radio Disney's Totally 10 Birthday Concert*, she was excited but definitely had the jitters. Miley had never performed for an audience of that size, so naturally she was feeling the butterflies. She knew that if she could just get through the first song, she'd be fine. And, of course, she was.

During her first couple of shows, Miley got nervous when she grabbed some fans' hands, and they didn't let go. She probably felt as if she was going to go flying into the audience. Not to worry – she stayed onstage.

With live performances, Miley loves having the energy and excitement of the audience to really pump her up. It is so much fun for her when the audience sings and dances along with her. 'I love looking out in the crowd and seeing someone sing along with the lyrics because it helps me not forget the lyrics even if I'm nervous.'

See, even big stars can catch a case of the nerves.

chapter 11
A Starring Role Model

If you're a star with a hit TV show and chart-busting CDs, you're probably going to find your face plastered over every teen mag. So it's no wonder that girls everywhere are going to look up to you. They will follow your every move, track what you wear, know where and what you eat, and who you hang with. Basically they are going to know everything about you.

There's lots of pressure put on teenage stars. You have to literally watch your every step. As a teen star, you wouldn't want to do anything that can be at all construed as being over the edge. You need to walk the straight and narrow.

But people have been obsessed with stars since the beginning of time, right? Ask your parents and grandparents about Elvis (who made teenage girls faint) or the Beatles (who made girls cry) or David Cassidy (who plastered many a wall). What's different about star obsession today?

Today, teens can worship their stars 24/7 – you can watch them on TV, you can download them on to your iPod, you can get fan club alerts blasted to your computer and your mobile phone. Today's teens feel closer to their favourite celeb than ever before. Some have even come to think of their star as their close personal friend.

Chances are that Miley's not your bud, but she is the kind of girl you'd want to be friends with. And the kind of girl you can look up to as well.

Miley is totally aware of all the social pressures that have been put on her. As a middle child in her family, she's always been looked up to by her younger siblings. The younger family members have always asked Miley for advice, which she is ready and willing to dole out. Miley is a great role model for her siblings – they can see that her success has certainly not gone to her head. She is still the honest, down-to-earth sister they know and love. Miley can feel confident that her parents have raised her right and have taught her how to be a good person.

Billy Ray knows all too well the pressures that come with the biz. And he has cautioned Miley to watch out for the good as well as the bad. Billy Ray's also confident that Miley won't be a wild teenager who's always getting into trouble. 'I see her being Miley Cyrus,' he told *USA Today*. 'She will never be somebody else. She's got her own thing. I think she takes and borrows and hints at a little bit of a lot of people . . . but she's her own person.'

Miley knows that Billy Ray has been a good role model for her. And neither of her parents give her the star treatment at home, which keeps her grounded. Like any other kid, Miley still has to make her bed and clean her room!

Miley has learned from her dad to treat her fans with respect. On more than one occasion, when growing up, Miley saw her dad get hounded by fans during family time, yet Billy Ray always made time for them. He would tell Miley, 'These people are supporting you. Be good to them.' Dad has certainly taught Miley well.

On 13 July 2004, Miley was attending a fan club event for Billy Ray that was held during the CMA Music Festival in Nashville. In the middle of the event, Billy Ray and Tish surprised their daughter with a pink Daisy Rock guitar. What was so special about that? Well it just so happens that the Daisy Rock Girl Guitars company was making Miley their youngest endorsee ever.

The mission of Daisy Rock, which is the only guitar company to manufacture guitars specifically for girls, is to empower young girls to play music and reach their goals. Miley's drive and ambition certainly fit the bill. 'When my wife, Tish, and I learned about Daisy Rock Guitars for Girls, we knew this was the perfect guitar and attitude for Miley,' Billy Ray said.

And one more thing: if you look at a Daisy Rock guitar, you'll notice that they're bright and sparkly – just like Miley!

chapter 12

Miley Style

No matter if it's preppy, goth, sporty, glam or funky, everyone has their own style. In Miley's case, however, she needs to have three fashion IDs – as Miley Stewart, as Hannah Montana and as Miley Cyrus. How is she able to keep them straight? Simple – she's a pro!

As Hannah Montana, plain is definitely not the name of the game. Hannah loves bling and everything that sparkles. From her dazzling clothes to her sparkly make-up, Hannah really shines. Wanna dress like Hannah? Here's a shopping list:

- ♥ **Hair:** Blonde wig (the wig that Miley wears as Hannah is *really* heavy – in fact, there are times when Miley's onstage that she's afraid it will fall off!)

- **Shirts**: A long, flowy antique-looking blouse, a sheer top with a cami underneath, a studded tank top

- **Dresses**: Definitely mini!

- **Jackets**: Anything cropped, anything with rhinestones, a distressed-denim jacket

- **Shoes**: Cowboy boots, suede boots, leather boots

- **Trousers**: Leggings, skinny jeans

- **Accessories**: A colourful glittery scarf, a beaded necklace, long chain necklaces

Even though the offscreen Miley readily confesses that she's a shopaholic, she has a really down-to-earth style. On her tour bus, Miley can be found wearing sweats, a hooded tee and Uggs. And on a photo shoot for *Popstar!* magazine, Miley showed up wearing 'Pink' Victoria's Secret sweats and a hoodie. 'I don't always go for clothes that are the most expensive,' she told *Teen Magazine*. 'It doesn't matter how little something costs. I [recently] got six-dollar shoes, and I was like, "Yeah." ' In fact, Miley counts American high-street shop Target as one of her fave stores! Miley loves Target because she can get clothing that's not too expensive, yet it's trendy. That way, you don't feel like you've wasted your money if what you've bought goes out of style in another two weeks!

Miley's always willing to take risks when it comes to fashion. She's not one to follow the latest fashion trend. Instead, she likes to be a trendsetter. Sometimes, Miley picks out a top and trousers that at first she thinks look really bad together. But once she puts them on and accessorizes, they look great! Miley's always telling people to do their own thing when it comes to fashion. Who knows – you may be starting a fashion trend of your own.

But, like lots of teens, Miley isn't always confident about her looks. She spends many hours in front of the mirror – and she doesn't always like what she sees! She complains about her hair, her nose and her teeth. But then she'll snap out of it, and her self-confidence shines through and she tells herself that she's beautiful.

Sometimes when she pulls together an outfit, she complains that it is ugly. Miley knows how hard it can be to pull an outfit together and readily admits that it's a lot easier when you have a stylist helping you get ready. She's lucky and she knows it.

In an interview with *Girls' Life Magazine,* Miley let loose a little secret: she hates getting dressed up. If you were to see her at red-carpet events, she'd probably be holding her shoes. After all, stilettos can be hard on a girl's feet! 'If I could go to premieres in my sweats, I would! If you wear baggy things and just put a little T-shirt with it, you'll look cute. A girl's outfit doesn't have to be, you know, everything all out there.'

Like her alter ego, Miley likes wearing jewellery. She likes necklaces and earrings, but she adores bracelets. She wears a charm bracelet that her mom made for her, as well as two bracelets that fans made her. And she never takes them off. In some photos of Miley, you won't see her bracelets, but that's because they've been airbrushed out (a little trick that the fashion industry uses when they don't want you to see something!). One of Miley's bracelets is a plastic band, like the kind you get at a water park. When she first had it, it was orange. Now it looks like a strand of grey string. Her mom thinks it's pretty nasty, but Miley refuses to take it off. Miley also has a bracelet that says 'live and love' that she got from a friend. But the piece of jewellery that is the most special to Miley is a ring. In some photos, you can see her wearing it on her right ring finger. The ring, which basically looks like a plain band, was originally two rings that her dad gave her mom. As a gift for one Valentine's Day, Billy Ray had the rings made into one and gave it to Tish. Tish then gave it to Miley. How sweet!

When it comes down to it, the fashion style of

the real-life Miley Cyrus and TV's Miley Stewart is pretty similar. Sure, Miley has to get dressed up when she goes out in public, but when she's off the set, casual clothes are just fine. Here's a shopping list that covers the styles of *both* Mileys:

- **Shirts**: Cotton tanks, short- and long-sleeved tees, tunics, camis, hoodies, a white lacy button-down blouse

- **Dresses**: A slip dress, a flowy minidress to go over leggings

- **Jackets**: Sweatshirts, a cropped knit sweater, a jean jacket, a basic black blazer

- **Shoes**: Canvas trainers, leather boots, dressy sandals, flip-flops

- **Trousers**: Skinny jeans, basic jeans, army pants, drawstring pants, sweats, leggings

- **Accessories**: Lots of bracelets, simple chokers, a western leather tote

While most teens like Miley know that they have to eat well in order to look healthy, Miley likes to dive into junk food every now and then. But, hey, who doesn't? Some of her favourite foods – if you can really call them food – are gummy bears and cookie dough. Her mom doesn't really think Miley should eat cookie dough, since it contains raw eggs, which could make you sick, but Miley tells her mom not to worry. A typical teenager's response! And when it comes to fast-food catering that's often offered to Miley on a photo shoot, she'd much rather have a fast-food meal.

No matter what she eats, no matter what she wears, the verdict is in: fans love Miley inside and out!

chapter 13

Get Miley's Number

Miley is probably number one on your list of favourite stars. And if you had to rate her on a scale of one to ten, you'd most definitely give her a perfect ten. So you'd probably be surprised to hear that Miley's actually a one, at least according to numerology.

Numerology is a practice built on the statement of the ancient Greek philosopher Pythagoras who said, 'The world is built upon the power of numbers.' According to this theory, all things, including names, can be reduced down to a number in order to figure out personalities, destinies and fortunes of individuals.

According to numerology, each person's personality fits into one of nine categories. In order to figure out someone's number, you have to match up each letter in his or her name to a particular number on a numerology chart.

How did we figure out that Miley is a one? First we wrote out all the letters in Miley's full name. But there's a catch here: you need to use the name that is written on your birth certificate. So we couldn't use Miley. We used Destiny Hope Cyrus. Then we matched the letters to the numbers on this chart:

1	2	3	4	5	6	7	8	9
A	B	C	D	E	F	G	H	I
J	K	L	M	N	O	P	Q	R
S	T	U	V	W	X	Y	Z	

First, let's add up the numbers in DESTINY: $4 + 5 + 1 + 2 + 9 + 5 + 7 = 33$. Next, we have to get the 33 down to a single digit, so we add up $3 + 3$ to get 6. Remember that number.

Next, let's look at HOPE: $8 + 6 + 7 + 5 = 26$. To get 26 to a single digit, add $2 + 6$ to get 8. Remember that number.

Finally, let's add up CYRUS: $3 + 7 + 9 + 3 + 1 = 23$. To get 23 to a single digit, add $2 + 3$ to get 5. Remember that number.

Now let's add up the three numbers you remembered: $6 + 8 + 5 = 19$. To get 19 to a single digit add $1 + 9$ to get 10. To get 10 to a single digit add $1 + 0$ to get 1. That's the answer! Miley is a 1 on the numerology chart. But what does that mean?

It means that Miley struck the numerological jackpot! Number 1 is one of the most powerful numbers in numerology because it is the leader of all numbers. Ones like Miley make great leaders because they are independent and charismatic. Thanks to her charismatic personality, Miley has great stage presence and her fans love watching her perform. She's also a big trendsetter for other girls her age. She's not afraid to take risks with her clothes and accessories or to try something new, and her fans are always quick to follow her lead.

Ones are also known for their creativity and

originality. So it's no wonder Miley has been so successful as an actress and singer. Her creative nature allows her to get into character, even in the most bizarre situations – like when she had to dress up as the school's mascot in an episode of *Hannah Montana*. It must have been hard to act while wearing a huge, smelly pirate head, but Miley had no problem! Her originality comes shining through in her music, too. Miley is becoming an accomplished songwriter. She uses her real-life experiences to inspire new lyrics and melodies. We can't wait to hear more Miley originals!

Number ones are extremely self-confident, self-reliant and disciplined – all traits that Miley has always had. When someone has self-discipline, she is able to correct, or regulate, herself in order to improve upon what she's doing. As a cheerleader, Miley must have had to constantly strive to improve the routines she was working on. The same probably held true for dancing. And when you're trying to break into showbiz, you must constantly work on your auditioning skills in order to land a part. Not to mention, you need confidence in order to make it through audition after audition without getting discouraged. Through Miley's great self-discipline and confidence, she was able to get the part of Hannah.

You can figure out your own numerology, too. Just add up the letters in your name. Who knows? Maybe you and Miley are numerological twins!

Number **ones** are a lot like Miley – and they make great leaders! People who are number ones are creative, independent and original. Number ones are extremely self-confident and self-reliant. Although number ones can be very generous, they have to be careful not to become too self-obsessed.

A number **two** is almost the complete opposite of a number one. They are not interested in becoming leaders. They are fair and always look at both sides of a situation before jumping to a conclusion. Twos are very gentle and patient and supportive of others, and they are able to easily empathize with other people's situations. Twos have to be careful not to let others take advantage of them.

Threes are very enthusiastic. They have a good sense of humour and are always ready to party. Threes are charming, creative and very friendly. However, threes can sometimes have a sharp tongue, so they have to be careful not to hurt others' feelings.

Fours are very practical and orderly people. They are hard workers who take their responsibilities very seriously. They are steadfast and often set in their ways, which could get them into trouble. Fours sometimes need to learn to be more flexible.

Fives love adventure and are always on the go. They love to explore, and their curiosity leads them to new places. People who are fives are never satisfied with the status quo; they crave change. Fives often start many different projects but don't always finish them since they are constantly looking for something new to do.

Number **sixes** are very nurturing people. Sixes are very loving, kind and gentle. They are full of understanding and see beauty in life. Since a lot of their decisions come from the heart, it can be difficult to reason with sixes.

Sevens often make great teachers. They are wise and deep thinkers. Sevens are loners and can be quite reserved. People who are sevens have to be careful not to withdraw from society too much.

People who are **eights** are born leaders who are high achievers and who are successful. Sometimes eights hold grudges, so they need to learn to forgive and forget.

Nines are very compassionate. They are always helping others who are in need. People who are nines are very loving and generous. They are also extremely charming! However, they need to be careful not to force their beliefs on others who think differently.

chapter 14

It's in the Stars

Miley's birthday is 23 November, making her a Sagittarius, the ninth sign of the zodiac. People who are born under this sign are known for having a good sense of humour. They are also generous, open-hearted and compassionate. Along with Aries and Leo, Sagittarius is a fire sign. People who are fire signs are naturally warm people. They are also extroverted, active, dynamic and very energetic. They are seen as inventors and leaders.

A lot of these qualities fit Miley to a T! She certainly has a good sense of humour, since she loves pulling pranks on the set of *Hannah Montana*. Miley can laugh with people, and she can also laugh at herself, which is a fabulous trait to have. It would be no fun to have a practical joker around who couldn't be punked now and then, too.

Miley also has a big heart. She is a great friend to her pals on the set and she is still a loyal bud to her friend Lesley back in Tennessee. And Miley is the best sis to her siblings.

Always bubbly and smiling, Miley is certainly one dynamic girl. And the fact that she plays two roles on her TV show – three if you count her country cousin, has travelled a lot with her dad, toured with the Cheetah Girls, and more, must mean that she has tons of energy! When you see her perform onstage, she is one big dynamo. Her spirit is contagious, always bringing the audience to their feet.

Sagittarians are self-confident, optimistic and enthusiastic. Even after a boring day, a Sagittarius would be able to come up with a fun story to relate. Sagittarians are the incurable optimists of the zodiac. They often look at the sunny side of life. To them, the glass is always half full. Sags are very honest, but sometimes this trait can backfire when they say exactly what's on their minds and end up hurting someone's feelings.

Miley's optimistic attitude sure served her well when she spent all that time auditioning for the role of Hannah Montana. If Miley hadn't kept her chin up during that gruelling time in her life, who knows where she'd be today?

A Sag is often the life of the party, with people standing around her cracking up at her antics. Sags are witty conversationalists, often possessing the gift of gab. They are very outgoing and full of spirit. You can tell that Miley is a true Sagittarius, because, typical of her sign, she always has a smile on her face!

As a friend, a Sagittarius is someone you can count on. They are always there for you, through thick and thin. Although Sags can be very compassionate, they can have a temper. But don't worry, their rage doesn't last very long.

A Sagittarius is always preparing for what is yet to come in life. They are not content with the status quo, and are always looking for more. They are honest and hard-working, and they always need a challenge to keep them going. And they will always excel when faced with a challenge. This is true for Miley. She is not content just being a TV star and having hit CDs as Hannah Montana. She's released her own CD as Miley – Miley Cyrus.

Sagittarius, along with Gemini, Virgo and Pisces, is a mutable sign, meaning that they are changeable. Although some Sags can be constantly changing their minds, they are also very flexible and adaptable. Miley certainly needs these traits with her crazy schedule. In 2006 alone, she filmed a TV show, released a CD, toured with the Cheetah Girls, and made countless public appearances. There's no way she would have been able to accomplish all this if she were fixed in her ways.

Sags also have many interests. That's Miley again – the girl can act and sing. People who are Sagittarians also love variety. They hate anything boring – something that Miley's life is certainly not!

If you look at the symbol for a Sagittarius, you will see that it is an archer. But this is not any old archer, it's a centaur. The top half is a man and the bottom half is a horse. According to ancient Roman mythology, centaurs were intellects. People born under the sign of Sagittarius are clear thinkers and are always seeking out knowledge. The fact that the symbol for this sign is a hunter means that Sagittarians are always hunting for something new.

Like the archer, Miley aimed her arrow high. When she pulled back the bow, her arrow flew up, up and away. And it hasn't landed yet.

chapter 15

What's in a Name?

Destiny. Hope. Miley. Hannah. So many names for just one girl. Although Miley doesn't use Destiny Hope any more, they are still the names that are printed on her birth certificate. Miley's parents named her Destiny because they thought she was destined for greatness – and they were right. Here's a look at what Miley's given names mean:

Name: Destiny

Gender: Female

Origin: English

Meaning: This name has the same meaning as the noun *destiny* – something that has been decided beforehand. It can also mean *fate* – something that is unavoidable.

Name: Hope

Gender: Female

Origin: English

Meaning: The name has the same meaning as the noun or verb *hope* – to desire something and expect that it will happen or that you will be able to get it.

Even though Miley plays a character named Hannah on TV, lots of fans call her Hannah when they see her. But Miley doesn't mind. Here's a look at what the name Hannah means:

Name: Hannah

Gender: Female

Origin: Hebrew, English, French, German

Meaning: From the Hebrew name Channah, which meant favour or grace. In the Old Testament, Hannah was the mother of Samuel the prophet. The Latin version of this name is Anna.

Billy Ray gave Miley her nickname when she was a babe – it was shortened from Smiley. So Miley isn't a real name, right? Well, sort of. Miley is actually an Irish family name. It was derived from the word *muadh*, which has three meanings: noble and big and soft. Maybe noble could be used to describe Miley, but big and soft? Not so much!

chapter 16
Pop Princess

There's no doubt about it – Miley is the new pop princess. Some may think that the reason the first *Hannah Montana* CD debuted at number one on the US charts was due solely to the popularity of the TV show. This was *so* not the case. The CD has many merits of its own, which cannot be denied. The CD features well-written songs that give nods to teen pop, rock and country. The themes of having fun, being yourself and following your dreams that are found throughout the album speak directly to tweens and teens. And Miley's rich voice is infused with such personality! After listening to the CD once, you'll find yourself humming the tunes and singing the lyrics in the shower.

Miley, as Hannah, sings eight of the tracks. Also

featured on the CD are the Click Five, Jesse McCartney, Everlife and B5. On the last track, Miley sings a song as herself – a duet with her dad, Billy Ray.

Hannah Montana – track listing:

1. 'The Best of Both Worlds' – Hannah Montana
2. 'Who Said' – Hannah Montana
3. 'Just Like You' – Hannah Montana
4. 'Pumpin' Up the Party' – Hannah Montana
5. 'If We Were a Movie' – Hannah Montana
6. 'I Got Nerve' – Hannah Montana
7. 'The Other Side of Me' – Hannah Montana
8. 'This Is the Life' – Hannah Montana
9. 'Pop Princess' – The Click Five
10. 'She's No You' – Jesse McCartney
11. 'Find Yourself in You' – Everlife
12. 'Shining Star' – B5
13. 'I Learned from You' – Miley Cyrus and Billy Ray Cyrus

There is also a special edition of the soundtrack that has two discs. The first disc is the standard CD with thirteen songs. The second disc is a DVD with five music videos used in the show:

1. 'The Best of Both Worlds'
2. 'Who Said'
3. 'Just Like You'
4. 'Pumpin' Up the Party'
5. 'The Other Side of Me'

chapter 17

Fifty Facts at Your Fingertips

You're Miley's biggest fan. Here's everything you need to know about her, right at your fingertips:

1. **Given name:** Destiny Hope Cyrus
2. **Nickname:** Miley
3. **How she got her nickname:** As a baby, Miley was always smiling, so her dad called her Smiley, which was later shortened to Miley
4. **Alter ego:** Hannah Montana
5. **Birthday:** 23 November 1992
6. **Sign:** Sagittarius
7. **Hometown:** Franklin, Tennessee
8. **Present home:** Los Angeles, California
9. **Hair colour:** Brown
10. **Wig colour:** Blonde
11. **Eye colour:** Blue/green
12. **Height:** 5' 2"
13. **Father:** Billy Ray Cyrus

14. **Mother:** Leticia 'Tish' Cyrus
15. **Siblings:** Older half brothers, Christopher and Trace; older stepsister, Brandi; younger half brother, Braison; and younger half sister, Noah Lindsey
16. **Pets:** Miley has a dog named Loco that's with her in California, but back in Tennessee, she has seven horses, three dogs and two cats
17. **First time onstage singing:** When Miley was two, she was onstage singing with her dad
18. **First TV role:** Kylie on the PAX show *Doc*
19. **First movie role:** Ruthie in Tim Burton's *Big Fish*
20. **Fave spots on the set:** Her dressing room and the beach
21. **Posters on her dressing room wall:** Orlando Bloom, Keira Knightley, Kelly Clarkson
22. **Favourite sport:** Cheerleading
23. **Hobby:** Shopping!
24. **Jewellery she's never without:** A purple and white bracelet that was a gift from a fan, a bracelet from a water park, a silver ring that her dad gave her mom
25. **Favourite subjects:** Maths and creative writing
26. **Secret #1:** She can't keep a secret!
27. **Secret #2:** Miley needs braces, but they will be put on the inside of her teeth

28. **Best bud in Tennessee:** Lesley
29. **Celebrity buds:** Emily Osment, Mitchel Musso, Ashley Tisdale
30. **Best way to keep in touch with her friends:** Using her Sidekick phone
31. **Team on Disney Games 2006:** Green Team (the Green Team tied for second place in the competition)
32. **Musical influence:** Kelly Clarkson
33. **Idols:** Kelly Clarkson, Raven Symoné, Judge Judy
34. **Favourite TV show:** *Laguna Beach*
35. **Favourite movie:** *Steel Magnolias*
36. **Favourite actress:** Sandra Bullock
37. **Favourite book:** *Don't Die, My Love* by Lurlene McDaniel
38. **Musical instrument:** Miley learned to play the guitar a few years ago. She was given a Daisy Rock guitar by her parents
39. **Celebrity crushes:** Ryan Cabrera, Ashton Kutcher, Chad Michael Murray
40. **Comfy item on tour bus:** Elvis blanket
41. **Candy she likes to eat:** Gummy bears
42. **Type of food she likes to eat:** Fast food!
43. **Favourite snack:** Cookie dough
44. **Favourite cookie:** Sugar cookie

45. **Favourite drink:** Caramel Frappuccinos

46. **Five songs on Miley's iPod:** 'Beating Hearts Baby' by Head Automatica, 'California' by Copeland, 'Invisible' by Ashlee Simpson, 'Please Be Mine' by Jonas Brothers, 'It's Going Down' by Yung Joc

47. **Bands Miley digs:** Underoath, Copeland, They Said We Were Ghosts

48. **Favourite thing to do when she's not working (or shopping):** Curl up and watch a video with little sis, Noah

49. **What Miley put in a time capsule:** A picture of Beyoncé, because she wants to have a career like hers, and a picture of a dress that she wants

50. **Recording contract:** A four-record deal with Hollywood Records

chapter 18

Pop Quiz

Now you know absolutely everything about Miley Cyrus, right? Okay then, it's pop quiz time! (And no turning to the back pages to find the answers!)

1. **What would Miley be most likely to eat on a photo shoot?**
   a. An avocado and tomato wrap
   b. Chicken McNuggets
   c. A Caesar salad

2. **What big parade in New York City did Miley appear in?**
   a. Columbus Day Parade
   b. Veteran's Day Parade
   c. Macy's Thanksgiving Day Parade

3. **What colour is Miley's Daisy Rock guitar?**

   a. Pink

   b. Electric blue

   c. Fuchsia

4. **What is Miley's little sister's name?**

   a. Noa Lizzie

   b. Noah Lindsey

   c. Nikki Lesley

5. **What's the name of Miley's hometown?**

   a. Franklin

   b. Flatwoods

   c. Francis

6. **Which team was Miley a member of for the 2006 Disney Channel games?**

   a. Green

   b. Red

   c. Blue

7. What is the name of Miley's dog?

    a. Coco

    b. Loco

    c. Lucky

8. Who has been Miley's singing influence?

    a. Beyoncé

    b. Kelly Clarkson

    c. All of the above

9. How many tracks are on the *Hannah Montana* CD?

    a. 11

    b. 14

    c. 13

10. With whom has Miley signed a recording deal?

    a. Hollywood Records

    b. Mercury Records

    c. Sony

Answers: 1. b, 2. c, 3. a, 4. b, 5. a, 6. a, 7. b, 8. c, 9. c, 10. a

chapter 19

Where to Catch Miley

Miley's sure been one busy girl. From the long hours spent filming her TV show, to the forty-city Cheetah Girls tour, to the countless appearances on television and radio, to lots of photo shoots, anyone else would probably be totally wiped out. Miley must get tired at times, but she loves what she's doing so much, she doesn't want to stop.

In case you haven't been able to catch Miley in person, you can always find her if you flip through a teen mag – and lots of times, she's on the cover! You can also catch up on what Miley's been doing by surfing the Net. But a word of caution here: always be careful when you're online. Never give out any kind of personal information – like your name, address, the name of the school you go to, or the name of your sports team. And never, ever set up a meeting with someone you meet online. Downloading pictures from an unknown source is another no-no.

When you're surfing the Net, you have to remember that not everything you read is true. It's smart to take in all the info with a grain of salt. There are lots of people creating websites out there, and some of their information can be exactly that: created. Before you go online, get permission from a parent or another adult in your home. And remember, websites are constantly coming and going, so if your favourite one disappears, don't worry – there'll be another one to take its place!

Miley Cyrus Official Site

mileycyrus.com

Miley Cyrus Tribute – a fan site

miley-cyrus.com

Miley Fans

mileyfans.net

Hannah Montana Official Site

psc.disney.go.com/disneychannel/

hannahmontana/index.html

chapter 20

There's More to Come

The underlying message in *Hannah Montana* is that celebrity is not to be confused with real life – that happiness comes when you stay true to yourself. This very theme is what drives Miley's life. Although she is practically an overnight sensation, she has stayed true to herself. Miley knows that Hannah is a fictional character. She is well aware of the fact that when she toured with the Cheetah Girls, many of the fans were cheering for the fictional Hannah.

Who is Miley Cyrus? She is a teenager, who with virtually no professional acting experience is the star of one of the hottest shows on Disney. She is a teenager, who with a limited singing and performing résumé has two bestselling albums. So far, her accomplishments have been mainly based on *Hannah Montana*. Sure, Miley is super-talented. Otherwise, all of this would have been impossible to pull off.

With all this good fortune, Miley has been able to stay grounded. She is still the bubbly girl from a farm in Franklin, Tennessee.

What did Miley do next? With a four-album deal with Hollywood Records signed, Miley released *Hannah Montana 2: Meet Miley Cyrus* in June 2007 – it was a number-one hit and sold over three million copies! This is her first CD as Miley Cyrus, not Hannah Montana, and the music is different from the tunes on the *Hannah* CD. The reason? Miley wanted to showcase Miley Cyrus, not Hannah Montana. 'It's got a little bit of a rock vibe and two songs have a kind of miniature rap,' Miley told a reporter. 'I'm well aware that I can't rap to save my life, but getting to have fun with that and kind of do cute little raps is fun.'

With another album releasing in 2008 and a Hannah Montana movie due out in 2009, Miley, we're sure you can do *anything* you put your mind to!

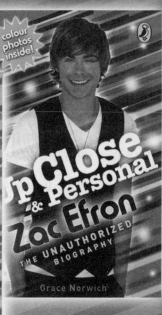